# Feeding Lac ,

*Also by Molly Goodland*

EVENING ON EXMOOR
GROWING WILD ON EXMOOR (writing as Molly Richards)

# Feeding Lady Winifred's Cats

Molly Goodland

RARE BOOKS AND BERRY

This edition first published in 2009 by

Rare Books and Berry
High Street, Porlock,
Minehead, Somerset
TA24 8PU

www.rarebooksandberry.co.uk



A CIP catalogue record for this title is
Available from the British Library

ISBN 978-0-9557119-5-4

Designed and typeset in Mrs Eaves Roman at
Alacrity, Sandford, Somerset

Printed and bound by
BAS Fine Art Printers, Amesbury

*For Jenny*

*who set me going*

# Acknowledgements

Special thanks to Rosemary Burnett and Giles Goodland
for all their help and encouragement

# Contents


| | |
|---|---|
| The Early Amazement | 11 |
| Polly Amber | 12 |
| Vinegar | 13 |
| Vile Child | 14 |
| Knitting | 15 |
| The Carver | 16 |
| Bound to Fall | 17 |
| Taking It | 18 |
| Tom | 19 |
| About Windscreen Wipers | 20 |
| Alice | 21 |
| Feeding Lady Winifred's Cats | 22 |
| Hope Deferred | 24 |
| North Hill | 25 |
| Melancholia | 26 |
| Assessment | 27 |
| Somersault | 28 |
| Smoke | 29 |
| Mismatch | 30 |
| Missing a Turning | 31 |
| Ordinary People | 32 |

The Right Medium 33
Off Road 34
Wren in December 35
First Grandchild 36
Outing 37
View from Below 38
Slow Worms 39
Weeds 40
Rape 41
Confinements 42
Choosing 43
Gathering Walnuts with Gretel 44
Rosemary's Chalet 45
Aging Cockalorum 46
Hills of Home 47
Old Timer 48
Chiffchaff 49
Time to Go 50
How Many Steps 51
Old Age Cocktail – My own recipe 52
Will it be Winter? 53

# The Poems

# The Early Amazement

After the first few weeks only the rain
kept us indoors, arms wound close
to our bodies, swaddled in shawls,
watching, intently listening,
enjoying the motion of pram wheels
along rutted lanes.

Left in the garden, in sight of the window,
we watched leaves dancing in the sky,
becoming aware; these first meaningful
months in the drama of autumn were like
a clearing in the mist
exposing a bright world.

Looking at a hand escaped from the shawl,
holding it to the sky, moving it
finger by finger, not yet able
to make a fist.

# Polly Amber

Polly Amber rides her horse
at two o'clock in the morning
over the heather and over the gorse
to see if the frogs are spawning.

She carries a jam jar under her hat
and laughs out loud at the weather
with strings and a net and her old pet cat
tucked up in a flap of the leather.

When she gets to the water's edge
she ties up her horse to a tree
and tosses her cat to the highest ledge
to see what she can see.

But all puss sees in the water black
are the silver reflections of stars.
The moon as well stares steadily back
above the planet of Mars.

## Vinegar

Mr and Mrs Snerdly-Bob were such an ugly pair,
they trailed their limbs in vinegar, never sought the air.

They multiplied their long-long tails
and moved to larger quarters,
for Mr and Mrs Snerdly-Bob
had many sons and daughters.

And all the little Snerdly-Bobs,
who were always pretty fickle,
starting life in vats of wine,
have ended up in pickle.

# Vile Child

One morning Gareth Lymphney-Sage
awoke in such a towering rage.

He took a saw and then an axe,
chopped at an oak and then an ash.
He trampled on the flowerbed,
locked his mother in the garden shed,
from where she sat and thought awhile.

This child, I think, is pretty vile.
He really must be made to see
you never ever bash a tree.

# Knitting

I liked the preparation, being taken to the shop;
selecting a pattern, choosing the colours
which hung in loops along the shop wall.

I liked standing arms akimbo, thumbs up,
while loosely-coiled skeins were hung
from hand to hand, and you unwound me
into tight and colourful balls
to roll about on the red-tiled floor.

And the click-clack of the needles,
knowing you were there, absorbed
in making me a rainbow jersey.
Your life turned for the time
into a bright pattern.

## The Carver

Each day at the head of the table
he stood sharpening his knives
on a steel. The dark room lit
with flashing light.

We sat in silence, waiting to begin.

## Bound to Fall

There she would be, with her mother-hen
clucks, without time for the little things in life.

Dispensing hard logic.
She knew what was needed to make us tough.

She, who could milk a cow, kill chickens,
swing a starting handle, ride horses, survive
a depression, six children, and a war
to end all wars. She had heard me coming.

Oh dear, have you hurt yourself?

I've falled down and hurted my knee!

How did you do that. You must have been
going too fast.

It's bleeding!

Nonsense. I can't see any blood.
Use your hanky. Next time don't go
so fast. If you do you are bound to fall.

## Taking It

Look at her, she can't take it.

Yes I can!

She's crying.

No I'm not!

Yes she is. Look at her everybody
she's crying her eyes out!

Now before you return (not
the original you, just another
of the same sort) with your grief
so raw, what to say, how to handle it?

I shall use acceptable words, wanting
to put it much softer, much stronger,
but shying away from any sentiment
likely to hang in the air.

I shall do what I have always done,
use plain words, look at the sky,
mention the clouds and wonder aloud
if rain is on the way.

# Tom

I do remember how you used to tease
and mimic and laugh like a man.

I do remember the happiness of you
up on the high fields, watching
the lambs in the sunshine.

I had forgotten the row, the time
you stumbled up that lane
where there was always too little light;
and forgotten too my fear,
that we might never see you again.

# About Windscreen Wipers

Six or seven of us packed with the driver
into an old Ford van, singing without
harmony, 'You can't get to heaven, in an old
Ford van, 'cos the Lord don't like you
as you am.' Stopping from time to time
to put more water into the engine from
the bottle you always carried.

And what about the windscreen wipers,
had they even been invented then?
We travelled in rain and blizzard,
with the window permanently open, while
you reached out to keep a clear patch
with what looked like a piece of lace
petticoat.

And we in the back, inventing verses
as we went, 'You can't get to heaven
in powder and paint, 'cos the Lord don't
like you as you ain't.'

How wild we felt, how cool, the roads
were almost empty then.

# Alice

When Alice with malice aforethought
danced in the nude on my forecourt,
I said, 'I find you too fat,
so please don't do that, come in
while I give it some more thought.'

## Feeding Lady Winifred's Cats

You would not find the cottage much changed.

The cart track too deep. Leave the car
and walk. You will remember;
as I said, not much has changed.

There is a small section where the wall
has fallen down on the sea side, replaced now
with wire netting, bits of fleece hang there,
and, surprised, a scurry
of sheep will run down the steep.

We sat there once, watching porpoises,
the can balanced on a flat patch of grass.

The gate into the woods needs to be lifted
the hasp still broken, close it after you.
Remember to take the top path, go quietly.

All along this level wooded walk
you will have the sound of the seas
(I loved it once) breaking on rocks,
a primitive breaking of everything not already broken.

Then we come to the stone cottage.

You are wearing the blue shirt, with sleeves
rolled up, and carrying the milk.

The cats are waiting to welcome us.
They wind themselves about our ankles
and I am watching
your bare arms stroking, stroking,
hearing the out-of-sight sea breaking, breaking.

## Hope deferred

Rarely troubling to make or repel
half-hearted advances, pigeons mope
in leafless trees, or sit on ridge tiles.

They seem to wait for something other
than this tag-end of winter.
With only the river running
black and slow, keeping things ticking over.

Will the days ever change, leap up, be bright
with blossom again, will I walk through woods
fresh-green and full of birdsong?

## North Hill

There is no view of the beach under
this stretch of the hill, foreground
to a choppy sea. A single small boat
rises and falls, going out of sight.

The colour-dead winter moor is littered
with weather-whitened stalks of gorse.
They stand out pitiable as sea bird bones
and one careless stride might land me
into the stormy sea.

# Melancholia

A sluggish rim to the sea
edges with yeasty scum
the plastic littered shore.

Waves far out ride high.
They are restless, coming in
all thrashing froth, giant washing
machine that will never reach this far.

Tomorrow, I tell myself, will be different,
I might be out there, riding high,
surfing with seagulls.

# Assessment

I was on time. We smiled a greeting,
he indicated my usual seat.
This was to be my last visit.
When he stood I stood
and moved to the couch.

Time to waste now, what was there
to say that had not already been said?
I watched the clock's hiccupping hands
move to the end.

I thanked him for his patience,
paid my final cheque. We informed
each other that I am now restored,
in balance, while he glances quickly
at the clock, and starts to clear the table.

# Somersault

Well ahead of me, yet easy
to pick out your shapes and colours
along the half deserted beach.

Not so distant now, my children
cavorting, yo-yoing away from
and always back to you, their voices
carrying clear: 'Look what I've found Granma!'

Grouping, stooping low over cupped hands;
your interest, as always, intent, informed.

So long ago, that sudden shift
and change of view, my
running to catch up, cartwheeling past
quick enough to catch your expression,
making the children laugh.

# Smoke

There were those times we sat
in easy familiarity, in a near silence
of tamping and rolling, wreathed
in blue grey smoke.

Seeing you in the mornings, shaving,
lathered in white foam, mirrored,
enjoying your first smoke
of the day. A habit, you assured me,
picked up in the army.

Then Gretel, with all the panache
of a Hollywood gangster, eyes in the distance,
deftly rolling, single-handedly her quick-lit
smoke, and like a gangster getting caught.

I think how idly we viewed each other
and each other's views. Life was good...

the self-deprecation, the smoke-laden tweeds,
the philosophers with cigars knowing we were
'all doomed', most of us gloomily agreeing
and that such a prognosis called for
another smoke, at least.

In the end, those of us remaining, gave up.
It was hard and left its scars. Conversation,
for me, is lumpy with things
I feel I should say, but cannot.

# Mismatch

Bright cushions scattered, pictures
rearranged, spaces in the bookshelves,
waiting, such a mishmash of me undone.

That picture of you half-way up
a mountain with your spaniel
where you looked so happy:
words are easy to transpose,

but did you ever look so happy after?

## Missing a Turning

No blending or blurring here today
where hills behind hills stand clear,
black-edged against a monochrome sky.

Yet I am lost again between valleys.

Trees point stiff fingers upwards, which
I interpret in my own way.

You had such an instinct for direction,
such a pleasure in maps, and a dislike
of signposts, however small, in walking country.

I felt safe then. You never got lost
nor would you have asked anyone for direction.

It's a long time now since I missed the turning;
found someone to ask the way; felt safe.

## Ordinary People

Going through life looking for the right
person, the right place. We might think
this is the one, but why here, surely this
cannot be the right place, things look
so different, dingy almost; and this
is not the one after all, not by a long chalk.

We take guidance, discover that places
and people can be made to suit,
see the advantages of being at peace.

Yes, this is the place, it kind of disappoints
being so ordinary. Yes, and this is the one.

# The Right Medium

Deep into untracked forest cold comes
parcelled in green air, lightly
perfumed with pine, stinging the nostrils.

What might be a squirrel moves silently
along high branches; here, no song birds
sing away the hours, no slanted sun rays
light up the ground.

My feet planted firmly amongst pine cones
lets me grow like a tree, waiting and listening
to the sea in the distance, shouldering
at jagged rock from a recent landslip,
smoothing the way for all to pass.

# Off Road

I have driven onto the moor
and stopped in thick fog.

Shapes of cattle loom up,
thinking my car a tractor
bringing their hay.

They push at the metal,
their breath stands out
drifting mist into mist.

They bawl and wait, fret and push,
until they hear the approaching tractor
and I lose them as they gallop away.

# Wren in December

Snow falls in large flakes forming a canopy
over rose bushes. A wren darts in, quick, quick,
taking insects from under red buds.

A strong breeze whirls the snow, wraithlike
turning so pure a white into dark shades.

I am wishing that I could paint.
I might get the snow storm, the right red
for the rose buds, but how could I capture
the energy and the speed of that small
wren's visit to my garden.

## First Grandchild

Out of the country,

out of wedlock,

out of kilter,

he with her

she with him

me with them.

Snapshots ...

Looking for a likeness,

new-tabbed baby

blissfully sleeping.

# Outing

My allotted seat is next to a woman
with a sad confiding face, who takes me
on a journey of death and betrayal,
seeming unable to stop until
her discomfort becomes mine.

I disinter some hoarded hurts, some
old injustices. Even-Stevens.

We relax and settle to the views,
and it as if we have met
for the first time again, with nothing
now we want to say.

## View from Below

It stood out in my mind
as a day when we might get
closer to an understanding.

Practising answers, pre-empting,
as I drove along, the inevitable
question of how old is too old.

We would be sitting at that high window
with a view of the hills, woods, and farms,
a small pond for the willow to weep into.

This narrow winding lane I'm on now
visible from a distance, but not to you.

How trite my painting for you
of brown-stained sheep stumbling
from the shelter of a rusty old shed;
or of winter horses galloping to hay
delivered under a heavy grey sky.

# Slow Worms

How truly slow they are,
those copper-coloured torques
coiled on the dark compost;
Shakespeare's blind worms
that 'do no harm'. They do not raise
their heads, hiss or spit venom.

I see them flinch under tea-bags,
potato peel and banana skin,
start to move down. For shame
I do not watch them go.

## Weeds

It concerns me that I have no calling
to dig in the garden, that I quite like
most weeds, and love the poisonous blue
monkshood that enjoys living here, admired
and avoided.

Above all I love the highly scented
old fashioned dark red rose, the way
it has bloomed, neglected, for more than
a hundred years. It is itself, as it was
in the beginning, for it, like the weeds,
will never revert.

## Rape

The path like a belt passes through
your blazing yellow dress, too bright
in sober English countryside.

Yet you further offend with bright
poppies suggesting armistice.

Later you are chastened by a summer
of heat and rain. You don then
herring-bone tweed, in muted shades
of cream and brown.

# Confinements

She is sway-backed and big-bellied
shifting her weight on tired legs.

Is it the pain that flattens her ears
or the memory of pain, brought close
by the sleek ungelded one, her last foal,
confined in the next paddock?

When the foaling starts his wild galloping
sends clods of dark earth falling.

Coming at last to a sliding halt
he watches as his mother reaches down
to her starred and gawky new-born,
already struggling to find his feet.

# Choosing

At the fruit stall, she moved
among the exotics, pressing
a peach with long white fingers.

Selecting a small pack of strawberries,
six kiwi fruit, a mango and lychees,
she caught my eye and smiled,

"Such choice these days," she said,
letting her gaze drift over
the colours with satisfaction.

I left her there, still selecting,
with my five pounds of potatoes
and a great hunger for change.

## Gathering Walnuts with Gretel

What you tried to tell me
was interrupted by thuds
as they fell to the earth.

Squirrels sprinted
about the ground, or moulded
their bodies half-way up
the trunks, watching
from upside-down with unforgiving eyes.

Preposterous words; you alive then,
I think I even laughed,
went on collecting, filling
first my pockets, then yours.

We walked out from the shadow of the trees
into the sunshine, which managed to shift
the chill which I had not noticed before.

# Rosemary's Chalet

You enjoy each spring
of cleaning, painting, window washing,
like playing dolls-houses again.
You cut the miniature lawn, trim the edges,
weed among the weathered shrubs,
bag up a litter of packets and plastic.

Then you lie down, stretching bare
arms and legs under the weak
and early sun, delighting in smells
of new-turned soil, fresh cut grass
and the sea.

You turn to me with a smile
and I notice a fine line of sweat
edging the line of your lips.

# Aging Cockalorum

Come sit beside me, I am bereft
and wear no artifice; what could
be the point.

You shout your sleek intentions
in a yellow waistcoat and dark
moustache, showing a face simply
more honest than mine.

In each swift appraisal
(which you will misinterpret)
every woman will know you, your smirk,
your posture, your spent genitalia,
and be moved to pity.

# Hills of Home

Seen above all the chimneys
that gentle patch of hill,
seeming to be all shades
of brown with a skyline frill
of conifers, nearly black.

But I know the cool air, perfumed
with gorse, and the heather so springy
underfoot, it will send the larks
lifting to the sky...

they will be singing and singing.
I can almost hear them from here.

# Old Timer

Who is the muddle-headed old one now?
The door-stop tripper over,
the handbag scrabbler, the loser of keys
and receipts, the birthday forgetter.

See the sand trickling, shards of quartz,
call them diamonds.

Where is that large portion of earth-brown
reality, the petty unhappinesses we inflict
and receive, the regrets, and the comfort
of ancient words? 'We are none of us perfect,
no, not one.'

## Chiffchaff

The hills around all black and white before a sky
full of snow. There is slush frozen on the pavement
out of town. Grandmother's footsteps, forward for two,
backward for one. Stop.

Then, from a garden by the church,
the chiffchaff
in a cold blink of sunshine, that call
again and again.

I stand to listen,
people want to pass. I say, 'That's a chiffchaff!'
as if by saying it, all birds would start singing,
bluebells and buttercups appear.

An older man cups his ear, apologises
and I am left listening.

## Time to Go

Long stripes of shadow cast far into the field
where horses breathe over the grass
intent only on the next mouthful.

Slow steps to a full belly.

A day's worth of warmth rests in the wood
of the gate. All along the hedgerow,
small creatures going home,
birds preparing to settle.

The woods turn dark.
The horses still graze, unaware of time
ever running out.

## How Many Steps?

How many steps will there be along
this slow creep to becoming nothing?
How many faces will you recall,
how many smiles, or remembered jokes?

You never thought to store and protect
so precious a thing, perhaps neatly
labelled in a compartment under the stairs.

But not up there in the unreachable
rafters of the almost unreachable
attic, which you sometimes feel
you have rented out to hoodlums

who might one day find it
and hold it against you.

# Old Age Cocktail

## (My own recipe)

Liquidise a depipped lemon,
add two spoonfuls of sugar.
Make a syrup of the above.

To this syrup add some desiccated passion,
a sliver of sensory deprivation,
some shredded confidence,
a smidgeon of frustration,
as much spirit as you can muster,
some of the soft stuff, not effervescent.

Go easy on the bitters, and throw in a handful of ice.

N.B. I use a stout old dumpy, for shaking.

## Will it be Winter?

Will it be winter
when I join those souls
forever roaming about the moor amongst
the dead and dying bracken; seeking
always seeking, rain-lashed
or swirled and lifted in cold air,
scattered like invisible seed

or briefly silenced under a covering of snow?

And will it be soon when I follow
wild ponies and deer among frozen
tracks beside stunted trees, pointing
rime-thick fingers to the sky?

Will there be nothing but soft whispering
through the sedge, gentle keening?

If you might pass along
the paths we once walked, and feel
a fleeting otherness, lighten your step
and think of me, perhaps with just
the ghost of a smile.